A Seat at the Table:
Recipes from the Heart

by

KJ Bradford

Table of Contents

Foreword **7**

Starters **8**

Main Dishes **20**

Side Dishes **32**

Sauces & Soups **46**

Desserts **54**

Libations **68**

Copyright © 2022 by K.J. Bradford
All rights reserved. All rights reserved. No part of this book may be reproduced in any form without permission from the author or publisher, except as permitted by U.S. copyright law.

Back Porch Publishing, LLC
10681 Grace Lake Drive
Fairhope, AL 36532

ISBN 979-8-9872693-2-9

Cover Design: Lindsey Nitzschke
Layout: Virginia Mathers

Printed in the United States of America

From the Chef's Seat

This book is inspired by the many
Sunday suppers I had at home
gathered around the table with friends,
sharing stories, laughs
and good food.

These recipes are a brief glimpse into
those wondrous days that I will always
cherish and hold near to my heart.
I love everyone that allowed me to love
through food and to be a presence
for such times.

There will always be
a seat at my table
for you.

Love Always,

KJ Bradford

Starters

Chicken Samosas

4 chicken breasts, poached and shredded

2 medium yellow onions, chopped

3 green onions, chopped

3 teaspoons kosher salt

3 teaspoons garam masala

2 teaspoons curry powder

2 teaspoons turmeric

2 teaspoons crushed chili flakes

1 teaspoon minced ginger

1½ tablespoons all-purpose flour

¼ cup white wine

½ cup chicken stock

2 packages of phyllo dough, thawed

2 sticks unsalted butter for pastry

In a medium size stock pot, place chicken, chili flakes, minced ginger, white wine and chicken stock. Poach chicken for 5 to 8 minutes, then remove the chicken breasts and allow them to cool.

Bring the liquid to a boil, reduce to a simmer, and let the liquid reduce by ¾ for about 20 minutes.

Once the liquid is reduced, slowly whisk in spices and flour. Simmer until the liquid has thickened, then allow to cool.

In a skillet, sauté the onions until they are translucent, then set aside to cool.

In a large bowl, combine shredded chicken, onions, green onions and ¼ cup of the thickened broth. Chicken should be moistened but not soupy.

Prepare the phyllo:

Take a sheet of the thawed phyllo dough and brush with melted butter, then top with another sheet of phyllo. Repeat process four more times.

Cut the sheet of dough into 6 equal portions. Fill each portion with 1 tablespoon of filling.

Moisten the corners of the dough and fold in half to make a triangle.

Brush each samosa with melted butter and bake in a preheated 375-degree oven until golden brown for about 15 to 20 minutes.

Serve immediately or at room temperature.

Grape Leaves

1 pound grape leaves, drained and rinsed

4 shallots, minced

2 cups basmati rice, washed under cold water and drained

1 cup Italian parsley, chopped

½ cup extra virgin olive oil

⅓ cup pine nuts

¼ cup dried currants or golden raisins

¼ cup mint, chopped

1½ teaspoons sumac

½ teaspoon ground white pepper

¼ teaspoon sugar

1 teaspoon salt

2 cups water, boiling

Zest and juice of one lemon

Sauté shallots in ¼ cup of olive oil. Once translucent, add pine nuts and currants and sauté for 5 minutes.

Add the rice and constantly stir for 5 to 10 minutes. Add the spices, then add boiling water and cook on medium low heat for 10 to 15 minutes. Let cool.

Once rice mixture is cooled, add herbs and lemon zest.

Fill each leaf with 1 tablespoon of filling, fold in the sides, then roll tightly. Repeat process until all the filling is gone.

In a large heavy pot, line the bottom with grape leaves.

Place the filled grape leaves in the pot side by side.

Add ¼ cup olive oil, lemon juice and 2 cups of boiling water to the pot. Cover with an upside-down plate, bring to a boil and simmer on low for 45 to 60 minutes until the leaves are tender and the water has been absorbed.

Let cool, then pack in olive oil and lemon juice. Leave at room temperature.

Roasted Lemon Hummus

2 whole lemons, quartered and seeds removed

4 garlic cloves

1 cup tahini

4 cups chickpeas, canned or freshly cooked and liquid reserved

1 teaspoon salt

¼ teaspoon pepper

½ cup olive oil

Optional garnish: chopped parsley or paprika, lemon zest

Roast lemons in a 400-degree oven for 15 to 20 minutes with the cut side down until they are slightly charred.

Remove the seeds from lemons.

In a food processor, combine lemons, garlic, tahini, salt and pepper. Pulse until mashed.

Place food processor on low and stream in olive oil.

If it's a little thick, add some of the liquid from the chickpeas.

Garnish with chopped parsley or paprika and lemon zest.

Company's Coming Spinach Artichoke Dip

12 ounces jarred artichoke hearts, chopped and liquid reserved

16 ounces cream cheese, softened

8 ounces mascarpone cheese

10 ounces grated mozzarella

5 ounces grated white cheddar

8 ounces parmesan

12 ounces prepared mayonnaise

1 tablespoon dry mustard

1 tablespoon garlic powder

1 tablespoon onion powder

1 tablespoon cayenne pepper

2 pounds frozen spinach

Salt and pepper to taste

Mix all ingredients together in a large bowl.

Adjust seasoning and bake in a 375-degree oven for 20 minutes.

Cheese Bombs

For Hollandaise:
4 large egg yolks

2 tablespoons water

2 tablespoons lemon juice

¾ cup unsalted butter, melted

¼ cup dry white wine

Dash of cayenne pepper

Dash of black pepper

For Coating:
2 bags of crushed barbecue kettle chips

¼ cup panko breadcrumbs

2 eggs

1 tablespoon water

1 cup all-purpose flour

For Cheese Mix
¼ pound feta, broken into small pieces

¼ pound shredded mozzarella

¼ pound smoked gouda

2 cups grated parmesan

In a medium sauce pot, heat wine, butter, lemon juice and water, then bring to a boil.

Once boiling, reduce to simmer. Whisk in eggs and cook for 5 minutes, constantly whisking until the mixture is the consistency of pudding. Remove from heat and chill for an hour in a glass bowl.

Once hollandaise is chilled, mix in all the cheeses until it looks like a cheese ball and refrigerate for at least an hour.

For the dredge, set up three separate bowls: one with flour, one with the beaten eggs and water, and the last with the crushed chips and panko.

Form the cheese mixture into deviled size balls. Dredge the cheese balls in the flour, then in the beaten eggs, and lastly in the chip mixture.

Fry in oil that has been heated to 350 degrees until golden brown in color.

Baked Crab Dip

1½ pounds cream cheese, room temperature

16 ounces prepared mayonnaise

4 ounces parmesan cheese

10 ounces grated smoked gouda

2 tablespoons Worcestershire sauce

2 tablespoons stone ground mustard

4 green onions, chopped

1 tablespoon garlic powder

2 pounds crab claw meat

Kosher salt and white pepper to taste

Mix all ingredients in a bowl until combined.

Place into baking dish and bake in preheated 425-degree oven for 15 to 20 minutes.

Smoked Catfish Rillettes

1 cup fennel bulb, diced

3 garlic cloves, roasted and mashed

1/3 cup extra virgin olive oil

1 teaspoon fennel seeds, crushed

¼ teaspoon gumbo file powder

1 teaspoon kosher salt

3 tablespoons lemon zest

8 ounces creme fraiche

¼ cup mascarpone cheese

1 tablespoon fresh lemon juice

2 dashes hot sauce

1 dash Worcestershire sauce

8 ounces smoked catfish

Smoked Catfish:
Soak wood chips in water for one hour, then drain.

Make a pouch out of aluminum foil leaving the center open so the wood chips release their smoke.

Preheat oven to 150 degrees and place fish on a rack.

Place smoker pouch on rack beneath the fish and cure for 8 hours.

Rillettes:
In a small sauce pot, place fennel, oil, fennel seeds and salt. Simmer on low heat for 30 minutes, then let cool completely.

Set up an ice bath, place stainless steel bowl in the ice bath, and mix together creme, catfish, hot sauce and Worcestershire sauce.

Transfer into nonmetal bowl and refrigerate from 1 hour to 3 days.

Before serving, let mixture come to room temperature for at least 30 minutes. Serve with crackers or crostini.

Steak Tartare

1 tablespoon truffle oil

1 teaspoon Worcestershire sauce

2 tablespoons olive oil

1 ½ teaspoons grain mustard

1 tablespoon chopped capers

1 tablespoon chopped shallot

2 tablespoons chopped parsley

2 teaspoons white wine

1 ¼ teaspoons salt

4 ounces beef, finely chopped

1 egg yolk

Mix all ingredients, then fold into the beef.

Use a 4-inch ring mold and pack the beef into the mold. Remove ring, then top with egg yolk.

Garnish with crostini, grain mustard, pickled onions and cornichon.

Deviled Crab Hushpuppies

1 cup all-purpose flour

1 cup cornmeal

1 ½ teaspoons baking powder

½ teaspoon cayenne pepper

¼ teaspoon onion powder

½ teaspoon garlic powder

1 teaspoon white pepper

½ teaspoon gumbo file powder

½ teaspoon salt

1 shallot, finely diced

2 teaspoons pimento peppers, diced

1 egg

1 ½ cups crab meat

1 cup whole milk

Mix all the dry ingredients in a medium bowl.

Stir in egg and milk until combined, then fold in crab and let chill for 30 to 45 minutes.

Heat oil to 350 degrees, scoop mixture into balls and fry 3 to 5 minutes until golden brown.

Remove from oil and sprinkle with salt.

Side Note: Hushpuppies can be made ahead and frozen. You can also add cheese, shrimp or lobster instead of crab.

Greens and Mushrooms Galette

2 tablespoons unsalted butter

½ pound baby portabella mushrooms

2 sprigs of rosemary

4 garlic cloves

¼ pound spinach, torn

¼ pound kale, torn

¼ pound arugula, torn

¼ of a red onion, sliced

1 ½ cups shredded gruyere

3 egg yolks, beaten

¼ cup half and half

1 tablespoon all-purpose flour

1 recipe of flaky pie dough

Kosher salt and black pepper to taste

Roast mushrooms, garlic, rosemary and butter in a large skillet in a preheated 425-degree oven for 15 to 20 minutes until golden and aromatic.

Remove from skillet and let cool.

Place skillet on medium high heat. Cook all the greens until wilted.

Once greens are cooked, drain in a colander positioned over a bowl.

Press the greens to make sure all the liquid has been removed from them.

Slice the roasted garlic and mushrooms and set aside.

In a medium size bowl, combine eggs, flour, half and half, cheese and salt and pepper, then set aside.

In the large skillet, place the pie dough that has been rolled out 10 inches in diameter.

Decrease the oven temperature to 400 degrees.

In a clockwise rotation, layer onions on the pastry, leaving an inch border from the edge.

Then, in between each of the onions, place a slice of the garlic. Spread greens on top of that evenly, then arrange mushrooms on top in a clockwise rotation.

Fold edges over the evenly spread cheese mixture on top.

Brush with egg wash and bake in a preheated 400-degree oven for 40 to 45 minutes. Remove from oven and let rest for 10 minutes, then serve.

Main Dishes

Garlic Rosemary Pork Chops

- 1 lemon, roasted and seeded
- 2 tablespoons fresh rosemary
- 2 tablespoons garlic powder
- 1 tablespoon onion powder
- 2 tablespoons white pepper
- 2 ½ tablespoons kosher salt
- ¼ cup olive oil
- ¼ cup white wine
- 4 center cut pork chops or pork ribeye
- 1 yellow onion

In a blender, puree all ingredients except onion.

Pour the marinade over pork chops and allow to marinate for 30 minutes to 4 hours.

Heat a medium sauté pan or cast-iron skillet on medium high heat.

Add 1 tablespoon of oil to the pan.

Cook pork chops 4 to 5 minutes per side.

Remove pork chops from skillet, then add onion and sauté for 3 minutes.

Add the marinade to skillet and cook for 7 minutes.

Return pork chops to the sauce and cook for 1 minute.

Serve over garlic rice.

Shrimp Provencal

3 Roma tomatoes, sliced

¼ lemon, seeded and diced small

½ red onion, sliced

4 garlic cloves, sliced

2 celery stalks, sliced

2 tablespoons capers, rinsed

1 bay leaf

2 tablespoons tomato paste

2 pounds shrimp, deveined with shell on

2 tablespoons unsalted butter, room temperature

16 ounces seafood stock

Heat a cast iron skillet on medium high heat.

Sauté onions and lemons for 5 minutes or just until softened.

Add garlic, capers and tomatoes and cook for 7 minutes.

Add celery, bay leaf and tomato paste, then add stock.

Bring to a boil then simmer for 15 to 20 minutes until slightly reduced.

Add shrimp and cook for 7 to 10 minutes, then serve hot.

Mussels with Tomato Brodo

6 pounds mussels, cleaned

2 bay leaves

6 tablespoons unsalted butter

3 leeks, chopped

30 ounces diced tomatoes

3 cups dry white wine

6 tablespoons chopped parsley

2 teaspoons kosher salt

1 teaspoon ground black pepper

14.5 ounces diced red peppers

4 garlic cloves, minced

In a pot over medium to low heat, melt the butter. Once the butter is melted, add leeks and cook until soft and translucent for about 5 minutes. Then, add garlic and cook for 1 additional minute.

Next, add tomatoes, peppers, wine, bay leaves and parsley and simmer for 1 hour.

Bring to a boil, add the mussels and reduce to a simmer. Cover with a lid and cook for 7 to 12 minutes until mussels open their shells.

Discard any shells that didn't open.

Garnish with parsley, rouille and grilled bread.

Snapper Alexander

4 snapper filets, blackened

6 tablespoons unsalted butter

½ cup red onion, chopped

1 ½ tablespoons flour

¼ cup white wine

½ teaspoon salt

¼ teaspoon white pepper

¼ teaspoon gumbo file powder

Dash of cayenne pepper

½ cup crab meat

12 Gulf shrimp, blackened

Melt butter in a large saucepan, then add the onion and cook until soft. Stir in flour and cook about 2 minutes.

Deglaze with white wine, then cook for 1 minute and add cream. Add seasonings and crab meat, then cook for 1 minute.

Cook snapper and shrimp in a skillet 3 to 4 minutes.

Serve fish over garlic rice or pasta, then top with sauce and 3 blackened shrimp.

Catfish with Fine Herbs Sauce

4 fillets of catfish

16 ounces seafood stock

¼ teaspoon garlic powder

1 teaspoon white pepper

2 teaspoons kosher salt

For Sauce:
4 to 6 tablespoons unsalted butter

1 teaspoon fresh tarragon, chopped

1 teaspoon fresh chervil or marjoram, chopped

1 teaspoon fresh parsley, chopped

1 teaspoon fresh chives, chopped

1 teaspoon dill, chopped

In a heavy bottomed saucepan, bring seafood stock to a simmer for 12 to 14 minutes before adding fish.

Season the fish with salt, pepper and garlic powder.

Add fillets and simmer for 10 to 12 minutes, then remove with fish spatula and place onto serving platter.

Sauce:
In a medium saucepan, heat cream for 5 to 7 minutes.

Once cream is warm, add wine and reduce for 5 minutes.

Remove from heat, add herbs and slowly whisk in the unsalted butter.

Check sauce for seasoning and adjust accordingly.

Pour sauce over fish and serve immediately.

Mirliton Stuffed with Crab Dressing and Pontchartrain Sauce

4 Mirliton/Chayote squash, halved and seeded for dressing

1 pound crab claw meat

1 cup all-purpose flour

1 cup cornmeal

4 teaspoons baking powder

½ teaspoon kosher salt

3 eggs

1 cup water

1 pound cremini mushrooms, chopped

½ yellow onion, diced medium

3 celery ribs, diced small

2 green onions, roughly chopped

¼ bunch parsley, chopped

1 teaspoon gumbo file powder

1 teaspoon Worcestershire sauce

1 cup heavy cream

Salt and pepper to taste

For Sauce:
¼ cup unsalted butter

8 mushrooms, sliced

8 medium shrimp, peeled and deveined

½ cup whipping cream

2 teaspoon Madeira wine

1 ½ teaspoons all-purpose flour

Salt and pepper to taste

Preheat oven to 375.

Slice squash lengthwise and bake for 30 minutes until tender, then set aside to cool.

In a large bowl, mix flour, cornmeal, baking powder, salt, water and eggs.

Bake in oven in a 9-inch pan for 25 to 30 minutes or until set, then let cool.

In a skillet, sauté vegetables until soft for 15 to 20 minutes. Add cream and cook for 5 minutes, then set aside.

Scoop out center of squash and mash it into the cooked vegetables.

In a large bowl, combine the cornbread, the vegetable mixture and the crab.

Stuff the mixture into the squash and bake for 15 minutes.

In a heavy saucepan, melt the butter, then sauté mushrooms for 5 minutes.

Add flour and cook for 5 minutes, then deglaze with Madeira wine.

Add heavy cream and simmer for 10 minutes.

Add shrimp and cook until the shrimp are pink throughout.

Ladle sauce over squash to serve.

Braised Beef Cheeks

4 garlic cloves, peeled

2 carrots, quartered

1 yellow onion, peeled and quartered

1/8 pound pancetta, diced large

2 1/2 pounds beef cheeks

3 tablespoons kosher salt

3 tablespoons coarse ground black pepper

1 teaspoon ground cloves

4 tablespoons Worcestershire sauce

1 pound cremini mushrooms, stems removed

2 dried or fresh bay leaves

16 ounces beef or veggie stock

1 cup water

In a heavy bottom Dutch oven on high heat, brown the beef cheeks, then remove.

Lower to medium-high heat, then add the vegetables.

Deglaze with Worcestershire sauce, then add the beef cheeks, spices, bay leaf and stock.

Bring to a boil, then simmer for 30 minutes. Place in a 300-degree oven for 4 hours.

Remove pancetta from stick and finely chop.

In a skillet, heat 1 tablespoon of unsalted butter, add pancetta and cook for 2 minutes.

Add mushrooms, 1/4 cup of stock and cook on stove on high for 2 minutes. Bake in oven for 10 minutes, then serve with braised beef cheeks.

Sausage Creole

4 links jalapeno kielbasa, sliced

¼ pound tasso ham, diced

½ yellow onion, sliced

3 garlic cloves, diced

2 tomatillos, sliced

1 Roma tomato, sliced

½ green bell pepper, sliced

1 teaspoon smoked paprika

⅛ teaspoon ground cinnamon

2 tablespoons Worcestershire sauce

3 tablespoons vodka

3 tablespoons tomato paste

3 cups chicken, beef or veggie stock

¼ bunch Italian parsley, chopped

Salt and pepper to taste

In a heavy cast iron skillet, sauté tasso ham until crispy for 5 to 7 minutes.

Add bell peppers and tomatillos, then cook for 7 minutes.

Add paprika and cinnamon and cook for 2 minutes, then add onions and tomatoes and cook for 5 minutes.

Add Worcestershire and vodka, stirring to mix, then add tomato paste and cook for 8 minutes.

Add stock and parsley, then simmer for 15 minutes. Add sausage and cook on low for 15 minutes.

Serve warm over rice.

Note: If sauce is not thickened, add roux slurry.

Roux Slurry:
1 cup all-purpose flour
½ cup oil
Whisk together.

Orange Chicken

For Sauce:
1 jar orange marmalade

1 tablespoon sesame oil

¼ cup soy sauce

2 tablespoons pepper sauce

For Chicken:
1 pound of boneless chicken thighs, cubed

1 cup cornstarch

Salt and pepper to taste

1 teaspoon ground ginger

2 cups vegetable oil for frying

In a medium sauté pot, combine all ingredients for the sauce and bring to a boil, then remove from heat.

Season chicken pieces with salt, pepper and ginger, then toss in cornstarch.

Fry until golden brown and thoroughly cooked for 8 to 10 minutes.

Remove from oil and toss in sauce.

Chicken and Biscuits

For Biscuits:
4 cups all-purpose flour

½ teaspoon baking soda

2 teaspoons kosher salt

2 tablespoons baking powder

4 tablespoons unsalted butter, melted

1 cup prepared mayonnaise

1 cup 7-Up

For Filling:
1 pound of mushrooms, sliced

1 yellow onion, diced large

5 celery ribs, diced medium

6 carrots, peeled and diced medium

2 green bell peppers, diced small

½ bunch parsley, chopped

3 pounds boneless skinless chicken thighs, chopped

1 tablespoon dried savory

1 tablespoon dried marjoram

1 teaspoon dried mustard

¼ teaspoon cayenne pepper

Salt and pepper to taste

4 cups half and half

Biscuits:
Sift dry ingredients into a large bowl.

Fold in wet ingredients until fully incorporated, then set aside.

Filling:
In a heavy bottom stock pot, heat a tablespoon of good olive oil, add onions and sauté for 5 minutes.

Add carrots, celery and bell peppers, then sauté vegetables for 15 minutes.

To the vegetable mixture, add seasonings, mushrooms and chicken, then cook for 10 minutes.

Stir in flour, making sure the mixture is evenly coated.

Add half and half and cook for 15 minutes, then remove from heat.

Pour chicken mixture into a 9x13 pan.

Spoon biscuit dough on top of the chicken mixture.

Bake in a preheated 375-degree oven for 15 to 20 minutes or until biscuits are golden brown and filling is hot and bubbly.

Chicken Cutlets with Mushroom Sauce

4 chicken breast cutlets

2 garlic cloves, minced

1 pound cremini mushrooms, sliced

1 tablespoon capers

1 tablespoon Dijon mustard

1 tablespoon Worcestershire sauce

16 ounces Marsala wine

4 ounces chicken stock

2 tablespoons all-purpose flour

For Dredge:
2 cups breadcrumbs

2 eggs plus ¼ cup of water

1 cup cornstarch

½ bunch parsley, chopped

Season cutlets with salt, pepper and garlic powder.

Dredge the cutlets.

Brown in a skillet with olive oil until just golden on each side.

Finish in 400-degree oven for 7 minutes.

Sauce
In a large skillet, heat 2 tablespoons of olive oil. Add garlic and capers, then sauté for 4 minutes.

Next, add in mushrooms and cook until they are golden in color.

Add flour and stir until the mushrooms are coated. Deglaze with the Worcestershire sauce.

Slowly add in Marsala wine and stock and cook for 20 minutes.

Finish with Dijon, parsley and fresh cracked pepper.

Add chicken to the sauce, allowing flavors to meld, then serve.

Baked Spaghetti

1 pound cooked spaghetti
(reserve 1 cup of pasta water)

For Sauce:
3 strips of bacon

¼ pound of pepperoni, sliced

4 ounces artichoke hearts, drained and chopped

1 package Italian dressing mix

3 tablespoons all-purpose flour

4 cups whole milk

1 cup heavy cream

2 cups grated parmesan

1 cup shredded mozzarella

1 cup shredded smoked gouda

¼ cup breadcrumbs

In a medium saucepan, sauté bacon in 1 tablespoon of olive oil until crisp.

Add pepperoni and artichokes, then sauté for 10 minutes on medium heat.

Add the flour and cook for 5 minutes. Once the flour is incorporated, whisk in milk and cream. Bring to a rolling boil and simmer 15 to 20 minutes or until slightly thickened, stirring occasionally.

Remove from heat and add half the cheeses and dressing mix.

In a large bowl, combine cooked pasta and sauce.

In a 9x13 baking dish, alternately layer the pasta mixture and the remaining cheeses.

Top with breadcrumbs and bake in a 375-degree oven for 20 to 30 minutes or until golden brown and bubbly.

Side Dishes

Green Beans with Lemon Sauce

2 pounds green beans, trimmed and blanched

2 garlic cloves, smashed

1 bay leaf

1 tablespoon kosher salt

For Sauce:
½ cup white wine

1 shallot, minced

½ lemon, roasted and seeds removed

¼ cup lemon juice

¼ cup heavy cream

¼ teaspoon ground white pepper

Bring a large pot of water, bay leaf, and garlic cloves to a boil. Once boiling, add salt and green beans, then cook for 3 to 5 minutes.

Remove from water and place in ice bath for 1 minute to cool down, then remove from the ice bath.

Sauce:
In a sauce pot, heat wine, shallot, and lemon juice on low heat just until warm through.

Remove from heat. In a blender, add wine broth, roasted lemon and slowly stream in heavy cream until the sauce is well blended.

Strain to make sure there are no seeds.

Place green beans in a 9x13 baking dish and top with the sauce.

Serve immediately.

SIDE DISHES | 33

Carrots with Hot Sauce Syrup

2 pounds carrots, peeled, cut into 1-inch pieces and blanched

For Hot Sauce Syrup:
3 cups brown sugar

⅛ teaspoon cayenne pepper

½ bottle of pepper sauce (Tabasco)

1 bay leaf

2 quarts water

For syrup:
Place all ingredients in a medium size pot. Bring to a boil and cook for 5 minutes, then simmer on medium heat for 15 minutes and let cool.

For carrots:
In a large sauté pan, add 1 ½ cups of syrup and heat over medium heat.
Add carrots, reduce heat to low and cook for 5 minutes until carrots are heated through.

Southern Baked Corn

1 pound frozen corn

1 cup brown sugar

2 cups breadcrumbs

1 red bell pepper, chopped

2 stalks celery, chopped

1 yellow onion, chopped

3 slices of cooked bacon, chopped

½ - 1 cup (as needed) chicken or vegetable stock

1 teaspoon gumbo file powder

1 ½ teaspoons garlic powder

½ teaspoon cayenne powder

Salt and pepper to taste

Preheat oven to 375 degrees.

In a large bowl, add all ingredients except for the stock.

Start with ½ cup of liquid. You want the mixture to be wet, not soupy. If dry, add more liquid.

Place into a 9x13 baking dish and cook for 30 to 45 minutes or until hot and bubbly.

Okra with Stewed Tomatoes

2 pounds fresh okra, ends trimmed and cut into pieces

1 yellow onion, chopped

4 garlic cloves, minced

28-ounce can stewed tomatoes

3 Roma tomatoes, chopped

2 tablespoons white vinegar

Salt and pepper to taste

1 teaspoon onion powder

1 teaspoon garlic powder

½ teaspoon cayenne pepper

2 tablespoons olive oil

In a heavy bottom pot, heat olive oil over medium heat.

Add garlic, onions and okra, then cook for 10 to 20 minutes.

Add spices and cook for 5 minutes, then add the vinegar and cook 5 more minutes.

Add fresh and stewed tomatoes and bring to a boil, then reduce to a simmer and cook for 15 to 20 minutes or until okra is tender.

Potato Latkes

2 large russet potatoes

1 large yellow onion, diced

2 large eggs

½ cup all-purpose flour

2 teaspoon kosher salt

1 teaspoon baking powder

½ teaspoon black pepper

Grate potatoes and onions and soak in water, then drain in cheesecloth.

Transfer mixture into a large bowl. Add the eggs, flour, salt, baking powder and pepper, then mix just until absorbed.

Make patties, then fry in oil 5 minutes per side until golden brown.

Enjoy immediately.

Clara's Collard Greens

4 pounds collard greens, stems removed, chopped and washed

1 smoked ham hock

1 yellow onion, chopped

1 medium jar diced pimento peppers

2 stalks celery, chopped

6 garlic cloves, minced

Salt and pepper to taste

1 teaspoon garlic powder

1 teaspoon onion powder

1 teaspoon gumbo file powder

½ teaspoon cayenne pepper

1 tablespoon apple cider vinegar

Water to cover

In a large pot, add greens, ham hock, celery, onion, garlic and water to cover. Bring to a boil and cook for 30 minutes.

Add spices, pimento peppers and vinegar, then cook on medium low heat for 20 to 25 minutes until liquid has reduced and the greens are tender. Adjust seasoning if needed.

Cheese Grits Soufflé

1 ½ cups grits

1 ½ cups whole milk

1 cup water

2 sticks unsalted butter, softened

3 cups grated cheddar cheese

8 ounces cream cheese

4 eggs, separated

2 teaspoons white pepper

1 teaspoons garlic powder

Salt to taste

Preheat oven to 375 degrees.

In a pot, bring water, 1 cup of milk and 1 stick of butter to a boil.

Once boiling, whisk in grits and reduce to low heat. Allow the grits to cook for 10 to 15 minutes or until thick, then let cool.

In a large bowl, blend together cream cheese, egg yolks, spices and remaining milk.

In a separate bowl, whip egg whites to stiff peaks.

To the cooled grits, mix in the cream cheese mixture and 1 ½ cups of grated cheese.

Fold in the egg whites into the grits being careful not to overmix.

Place into a 13 x 9 greased baking dish.

Top with remaining cheese and bake until golden and bubbly for 20 to 25 minutes.

Serve warm.

Farmhouse Biscuits

4 cups all-purpose flour

½ teaspoon baking soda

2 teaspoons kosher salt

2 tablespoons baking powder

4 tablespoons unsalted butter, melted

1 cup prepared mayonnaise

1 cup 7-Up

Preheat oven to 375 degrees.

In a large bowl, whisk together dry ingredients.

Add wet ingredients and fold until incorporated.

Refrigerate for up to 1 hour before rolling out.

Roll out ¼ - ½ inch thickness, cut with biscuit cutter and bake on an ungreased pan for 8 to 12 minutes.

SIDE DISHES

Sweet Potato Waffles

1 ½ cups mashed sweet potatoes

2 cups all-purpose flour

1 tablespoon baking powder

½ teaspoon salt

6 egg whites

¼ cup brown sugar

¼ cup melted butter

1/8 teaspoon ground black pepper

¼ teaspoon nutmeg

1 cup whole milk

Peel and cut 2 sweet potatoes and boil until soft for about 20 minutes, then set aside.

Whip egg whites into stiff peaks, then set aside.

In a bowl, combine butter, potatoes and milk.

Fold in dry ingredients, then fold in egg whites.

Cook according to waffle maker instructions.

Bucatini with Melon Sauce

1 pound bucatini pasta

1 cantaloupe, peeled, seeded and roughly chopped

2 garlic cloves

¼ cup white wine

1 ½ cups heavy cream

Salt and white pepper to taste

Cook pasta to al dente.

In a sauce pot, simmer melon, garlic, heavy cream and white wine for 15 minutes.

Puree in a blender, then strain.

Return to pot and reduce sauce by half.

Adjust seasoning. In a large sauté pan, add bucatini and sauce, then cook for 5 minutes.

Serve immediately.

SIDE DISHES | 39

Watermelon Feta Salad

Dressing:
2 garlic cloves, minced

1 teaspoon dried marjoram

½ teaspoon Dijon mustard

¼ cup red wine vinegar

½ teaspoon ground black pepper

½ cup extra virgin olive oil

Salad:
½ watermelon, peeled and diced large

½ pound feta cheese, broken up

¼ bunch Italian parsley, chopped

¼ bunch mint, finely chopped

¼ red onion, diced

In a large bowl, mix all the ingredients for the dressing.

Toss in salad ingredients and chill until needed.

Beet and Potato Salad

1 red beet,
peeled and diced large

1 golden beet,
peeled and diced large

3 Yukon gold potatoes,
peeled and diced large

4 eggs, boiled,
peeled and diced small

2 celery ribs, diced small

2 garlic cloves, grated

2 ounces
pimento peppers, diced

3 tablespoons
stone ground mustard

¼ cup prepared mayonnaise

¼ bunch parsley, chopped

Kosher salt and pepper
to taste

While wearing gloves, peel the beets and boil them until fork tender in separate pots so the colors won't bleed together. Drain and set aside to cool.

Peel the potatoes, then boil until fork tender. Drain and set aside.

In a large bowl, combine the remaining ingredients and chill for 30 minutes to allow flavors to develop.

Once chilled, gently fold in the potatoes and beets, then chill until ready to serve.

Buffet Potatoes

1 pound Yukon gold potatoes, diced large

1 red onion, diced small

1 jalapeno, diced finely

4 garlic cloves, minced

1 pint sour cream

½ cup unsalted butter, melted

10 ounces grated cheddar cheese

5 ounces grated smoked gouda cheese

2 ounces Pecorino Romano cheese

1 cup panko breadcrumbs

8 ounces cream cheese

1 cup heavy cream

8.5 ounces mayonnaise

2 tablespoons dried Italian seasoning

Kosher salt and white pepper to taste

Bring a large pot of salted water to a boil. Once boiling, add potatoes and cook them for 5 minutes. Drain and set aside.

In a large bowl, combine mayo, sour cream, heavy cream and cream cheese. Mix until blended.

To mixture, fold in cheddar, gouda, potatoes, onion, jalapenos and garlic.

Season with salt and pepper, then pour into a greased 9x13 pan.

In a small bowl, mix Pecorino, breadcrumbs and the Italian seasoning.

Top potatoes with breadcrumb mixture, then drizzle melted butter on top.

Bake in a preheated oven at 375 degrees over 45 to 55 minutes until golden brown and bubbly.

Orecchiette with Verde alla Crema

1 pound dry orecchiette, cooked al dente

5 cremini mushrooms, sliced

¼ yellow onion, diced small

4 ounces roasted pine nuts

3 garlic cloves, minced

¼ pound ground Italian sausage (optional)

1 small container of mascarpone

**Verde Sauce
5 garlic cloves**

1 bunch green onions

1 tablespoon capers

1 bunch parsley

½ yellow onion

16 ounces veggie stock

For the Verde sauce, combine all the ingredients in a blender or food processor, then set aside.

Cook pasta in salted boiling water according to package, then drain and set aside. Do not rinse.

In a medium oven, heat 2 tablespoons of good olive oil, then sauté onion, garlic and mushrooms until tender for 5 to 7 minutes.

If using meat, turn the heat up to medium high heat, then remove onion mixture and brown meat. Once meat is browned, add onion mixture and Verde sauce, then simmer on low heat for 20 minutes.

Once sauce has simmered, add in mascarpone and simmer for 5 to 8 minutes, then remove from heat.

Toss in the orecchiette and top with pine nuts and serve immediately.

Spaghetti Squash Casserole

1 large spaghetti squash, roasted

1 medium yellow onion, diced medium

3 garlic cloves, minced

3 celery ribs, diced small

½ jalapeno, diced finely

¼ pound baby portabella mushrooms, sliced thinly

¼ teaspoon ground turmeric

1 tablespoon dried parsley

5 tablespoons Worcestershire sauce

1 pound grated pepper jack cheese

1 pound ground beef

10 ounces breadcrumbs

1 (16-ounce) can diced tomatoes with green chiles

Split squash in half and remove the seeds. Roast in a 375-degree oven for 45 minutes to 1 hour until squash is fork tender, then set aside.

In a large heavy bottom Dutch oven, sauté onions until opaque and tender on medium heat for about 7 minutes.

Add garlic, celery and jalapeno, then sauté for 15 minutes.

Turn up to medium high heat and add your sliced mushrooms, then sauté for 10 minutes.

Add turmeric and sauté for 5 minutes, then deglaze with Worcestershire sauce and reduce for 15 minutes.

Add ground beef and cook until brown for about 15 to 20 minutes.

Add tomatoes and seasonings, then cook for 15 minutes.

Tighten up with slurry (¼ cup all-purpose flour and ¼ cup milk mixed together).

Add slurry and cook for 10 minutes, then remove from heat and set aside.

Take a fork and remove the insides of the squash into a large bowl.

Mix meat mixture into the squash, checking to see if seasonings need to be adjusted.

Stir in 2 cups all-purpose flour, then add into a 9x13 dish.

Top with cheese and breadcrumbs.

Bake at 375 degrees until golden and bubbly.

Cowboy Potato Salad

5 medium Yukon gold potatoes, diced medium

¼ red onion, diced small

1/8 cup neutral flavored oil (such as vegetable or canola)

½ red bell pepper, seeded and diced small

2 ribs of celery, diced small

1 bunch scallions, chopped finely

1 tablespoon capers, chopped

2 teaspoons apple cider vinegar

2 tablespoons stone ground mustard

¼ cup prepared mayonnaise

3 to 5 dashes of hot sauce

Kosher salt and black pepper to taste

3 hard boiled eggs, roughly chopped (optional)

Coat potatoes in oil and roast in a preheated 400-degree oven until fork tender for 40 to 50 minutes.

In a large bowl, combine all ingredients except eggs and refrigerate for 1 hour.

Once potatoes are cooked, turn off oven and let potatoes cool in oven for 20 minutes.

Add cold potatoes and eggs into the dressing, then refrigerate for 1 hour before serving.

SIDE DISHES

Sauces, Soups & Preserves

Apricot Blatjang

1 pound peaches, fresh or frozen

1 bay leaf

½ pound dried apricots

1 pound red onions, sliced

1 pound granulated sugar

3 tablespoons Worcestershire sauce

2 teaspoons chili powder

2 teaspoons salt

¼ teaspoon allspice

¼ teaspoon cinnamon

2 cups white wine vinegar

Soak apricots in the vinegar to rehydrate for about 1 hour.

Chop all the ingredients.

Place all ingredients in large stock pot and gently heat for 20 minutes.

Bring to a boil, then simmer on low heat for 1 hour.

Let cool, then put into jars.

SAUCES, SOUPS & PRESERVES

Cabernet Reduction

1 shallot, minced

3 garlic cloves, minced

½ cup red wine vinegar

1/3 cup chopped cilantro

2 tablespoons chopped parsley

2 tablespoons dried oregano

¾ cup olive oil

1 bottle cabernet

3 tablespoons beef base

¼ cup honey

Salt and pepper to taste

Roux to thicken

In a medium saucepot, combine all ingredients except the roux. Simmer for 20 minutes.

Pour all ingredients into blender and blend until smooth.

Return to stove, adjust seasoning and add roux to thicken.

French Onion Soup

16 yellow onions, peeled and sliced

8 tablespoons beef base

4 cloves garlic, minced

4 bay leaves

2 tablespoons herbes de Provence

3 cups dry white wine

4 quarts beef stock

1 baguette

1 pound grated gruyere cheese

In a stock pot with 2 tablespoons of oil, cook onions on low heat until caramelized, stirring occasionally for 3-4 minutes.

Add beef base, garlic, bay leaves and seasoning. Cook for 5 minutes to release aromatics.

Add wine and beef stock, then simmer for 30 to 45 minutes.

Adjust seasoning, then add roux. Simmer for 10 more minutes and serve in soup crocks.

Rouille

2 to 3 slices of stale bread, crust removed

3 garlic cloves, crushed

1 teaspoon fresh squeezed lemon juice

2 egg yolks

Small pinch of saffron threads

¼ teaspoon turmeric powder

1 cup extra virgin olive oil

1 tablespoon white wine

Salt and pepper to taste

In the bowl of the food processor, combine bread, garlic, egg yolks, lemon juice, saffron and turmeric.

Pulse until smooth, then slowly drizzle in the olive oil and wine. Process continuously until the mixture thickens.

Season with salt and pepper to taste.

SAUCES, SOUPS & PRESERVES

Jicama - Tomatillo Compote

1 tablespoon olive oil

1 medium tomatillo, diced large

2 tablespoons chopped parsley

¼ jicama, peeled and diced large

1/8 pound pancetta, diced small

2 tablespoons Dijon or spicy brown mustard

4 tablespoons apple cider vinegar

⅛ cup vegetable oil

3 tablespoons water plus ⅛ cup water

Salt and pepper to taste

In a large saucepan, simmer pancetta in ⅛ cup of water. Once the water has evaporated, sauté pancetta in olive oil.

Add Dijon mustard and whisk in, then reduce to low heat.

Deglaze with vinegar, then slowly whisk in oil and remove from heat.

Whisk in water, then pour over jicama, tomatillo and parsley mixture.

Use while still warm.

Pea Pesto

1 pound frozen English peas, thawed

1 shallot, sliced

5 garlic cloves, smashed

8 ounces parmesan cheese

4 ounces walnuts, toasted and chopped

1 bunch fresh basil

½ bunch fresh parsley

1 ½ cups extra virgin olive oil

For the peas, bring to room temperature; if still not softened, heat in simmering water.

In a food processor, pulse shallot, garlic and walnuts. Add peas and pulse immediately. Add basil and parsley, then pulse while streaming in olive oil.

Season with salt and pepper and refrigerate.

Salsa Verde

5 garlic cloves

1 (6-ounce) can whole green chiles

1 bunch green onions

½ yellow onion, roasted

6 cremini mushrooms, roasted

1 bunch cilantro

2 tablespoons capers

1 cup cherry tomatoes, roasted

3 pounds tomatillos, roasted

16 ounces veggie stock

Salt and pepper to taste

In a preheated 375-degree oven, roast all the vegetables for 15 to 25 minutes until they are slightly charred and aromatic.

In a blender or food processor, add all ingredients except for the liquid. Slowly pour in stock while blender is running to make a homogenous mixture.

Season to taste.

SAUCES, SOUPS & PRESERVES

Hot Sauce Syrup

1 chile de arbol

1 cup brown sugar

1 cup white sugar

1 tablespoon cayenne pepper

1 bay leaf

1 tablespoon pepper sauce

2 ½ quarts water

In a stock pot, bring all ingredients to a boil. Boil for 10 minutes, then simmer for 20 minutes.

Remove from stove and let cool.

Mushroom Pate

1 shallot, sliced

1 pound wild mushrooms

¼ bunch parsley

2 tablespoons bacon fat

3 tablespoons Madeira wine

½ cup water

Salt and pepper to taste

Sauté shallots, then once translucent add parsley and sauté for 2 minutes.

Add fat, then mushrooms and cook for 15 minutes on medium heat.

Deglaze with Madeira, then cook for 2 minutes.

Add water and simmer for 15 minutes.

Blend into paste and season with salt and pepper.

Serve with crostini.

Pickled Red Onions

2 red onions, sliced

1 cup water

½ cup red wine vinegar

1 bay leaf

3 tablespoons honey

3 teaspoons salt

½ teaspoon red pepper flakes

Place sliced onions into 1 quart container.

Heat remaining ingredients on the stove, then pour over onions.

Cover with lid and let cool.

Champagne Dressing

¼ cup honey

1 cup Creole mustard

1 teaspoon white pepper

1 tablespoon dried parsley

2 teaspoons salt

½ bottle of white wine

3 cups olive oil

Place all ingredients in a blender and blend until mixture is combined.

Desserts

Beignets

1 cup whole milk

2 tablespoons granulated sugar

1 - .25 ounce-package active dry yeast

1 cup warm water (110 degrees)

¼ cup melted butter

6 cups all-purpose flour

1 teaspoon salt

¼ teaspoon vanilla

Warm milk on the stove until it begins to bubble. Remove from heat and mix in sugar until dissolved. Let cook until lukewarm.

In a small bowl, dissolve yeast in warm water and let stand for 10 minutes.

In a large bowl, combine milk, yeast mix and butter and 3 cups of the flour into a smooth mixture.

Add salt, remaining flour or enough to make a soft dough. Knead, then place into a greased bowl, cover and let double in size.

Punch down the dough, then roll out onto a floured surface. Roll out ½ inch thick and cut into squares.

Fry in oil that has been heated to 350 degrees, fry until golden brown, then dust with powdered sugar.

Tiramisu Cheesecake

2 ½ pounds softened cream cheese	In a stand mixer, whip eggs and sugar until double in volume for 10 to 12 minutes.
8 ounces mascarpone	Add cream cheese and whip until smooth and creamy, then add mascarpone, yogurt, wine and vanilla. Mix just until combined.
1 ½ cups Greek yogurt	
6 egg yolks	Refrigerate mixture for 30 minutes.
1 whole egg	Slice cake into ¼ inch slices.
2 tablespoons sweet wine	Press cake slices into a greased 12-inch spring form pan.
1 ½ teaspoons vanilla	Pour filling into the pan and bake in preheated 350-degree oven for 1 hour.
3 cups granulated sugar	
¼ cup espresso	
1 frozen pound cake	

Topping

1 pint heavy whipping cream	Whip heavy cream to stiff peaks, then fold in the rest of the ingredients. Top off chilled cheesecake.
½ cup Greek yogurt	
¼ cup confectioners' sugar	
½ teaspoon vanilla	
½ teaspoon sweet wine	

Silk Chocolate Cake

Cake
2 2/3 cups granulated sugar

1 tablespoon strong coffee

2 ½ cups all-purpose flour

1 ½ cups unsweetened cocoa powder

2 teaspoons baking soda

1 teaspoon salt

2 cups buttermilk

1 cup vegetable oil

6 large eggs

2 teaspoons vanilla

Chocolate Crunch
9 ounces chocolate

2 cups Rice Krispies cereal

Frosting
4 ounces unsweetened chocolate

6 ounces semisweet chocolate

1 ½ cups softened unsalted butter

6 to 7 cups powdered sugar

1 tablespoon vanilla

4 tablespoons heavy cream

¼ teaspoon salt

Ganache
2 ounces dark chocolate

½ cup heavy cream

2 teaspoons corn syrup

Whisk together the dry ingredients and set aside.

In a separate bowl, whisk together all the wet ingredients.

With the mixer on low speed, slowly add the wet ingredients into the dry until combined.

Divide batter between 3 baking pans and bake at 350 degrees for 30 to 35 minutes or until toothpick comes out clean.

Let cool for 1 hour.

Crunch
Melt chocolate in a microwave safe bowl 15 seconds at a time.

Mix with cereal, then place on parchment paper and let cool.

Icing
Melt chocolate in microwave, then set aside.

In a mixer, beat butter until smooth and fluffy.

Add vanilla and heavy cream slowly.

Add chocolate and set aside.

To assemble the cake:
Fill each layer with the frosting, then chill for 30 minutes. Set on a wire rack and pour ganache over. Let the ganache set, then top with the chocolate crunch.

DESSERTS | 57

Red Wine Chocolate Cake

2 cups all-purpose flour

¾ cup cocoa powder

½ cup melted chocolate

1 ¼ teaspoons baking soda

½ teaspoon salt

1 pinch cinnamon

1 teaspoon vanilla

2 eggs

1 ¾ cups sugar

8 ounces unsalted butter, softened

1 ¼ cups dry red wine

Preheat oven to 350 degrees.

In a bowl, whisk all dry ingredients together.

In a large bowl, whip butter and sugar until light and fluffy. Add eggs one at a time and beat until incorporated. Add vanilla and mix for 2 minutes.

With mixer on low speed, alternate the dry mixture and the wet until just incorporated.

Bake in greased pan 35 to 45 minutes until toothpick comes out clean. Let rest for 10 minutes.

Mixed Berry Clafoutis

2 pounds assorted berries

½ cup granulated sugar

½ cup all-purpose flour

1 ½ cups half and half

2 tablespoons honey

3 eggs

Preheat oven to 325 degrees.

In a bowl, combine all ingredients except for the berries.

In a medium baking dish, place berries.

Top with batter and bake until golden brown for about 30 to 40 minutes.

Serve immediately.

Strawberry Cloud Cake

For Icing:
2 quarts heavy cream, whipped to stiff peaks

1 pound unsalted butter, softened

8 ounces cream cheese, softened

3 cups powdered sugar, sifted

1 teaspoon Jamaican rum extract

¼ teaspoon vanilla extract

For Filling:
1 pound fresh strawberries, hulled and sliced

16 ounces strawberry jam

8 ounces raspberry jam

For Cake:
1 ¾ cups granulated sugar

1 ½ teaspoons cream of tartar

¼ teaspoon salt

1 cup cake flour, sifted

12 egg whites, room temperature

⅓ cup warm water

1 teaspoon strawberry extract

Icing:
Whip heavy cream to stiff peaks and set aside.

Whip butter, cream cheese and flavorings until light and fluffy for 3 to 7 minutes.

Gently fold the two together and set aside.

Filling:
Remove the hull from the strawberries and slice thinly.

Combine the strawberry and raspberry jams.

Fold in strawberries and set aside.

Cake:
Preheat oven to 350 degrees.

In a food processor, grind sugar until super fine. Sift half of the sugar with the salt and cake flour. Set aside the remainder.

In a large bowl, whisk together egg whites, water, strawberry extract and cream of tartar. Slowly sift in sugar and beat on medium speed until medium peaks form.

Sift the flour mixture over the egg whites and gently fold until incorporated.

Spoon mixture into two greased 9-inch cake pans. Bake for 35 minutes.

Assembly:
Remove cooled cakes from pan and slice each into halves.

Place the icing into a pastry bag with a round tip.

Assemble the cake, making a circular piping of the cream about 1-inch thick. Fill the center with jam and repeat for remaining layers.

Chill cake for 45 minutes.

Frost cake with icing.

DESSERTS

Cream Pastry Dough

8 ounces cream cheese, softened

2 sticks unsalted butter, chilled

¼ cup granulated sugar

4 cups all-purpose flour

3 teaspoons ice cold water

In a food processor, pulse the flour, butter, cream cheese and sugar until it resembles pearls.

Slowly pulse in water until it forms a dough. Form into a disk and refrigerate overnight.

Apple Frangipane Galette

¼ cup butter, room temperature

½ cup powdered sugar

¾ cup almond flour

1 tablespoon all-purpose flour

1 large egg

⅛ teaspoon almond extract

1 package puff pastry

1 large egg and 2 tablespoons heavy cream for egg wash

2 medium apples, peeled, cored and sliced thinly

¼ cup granulated sugar

½ teaspoon ground cinnamon

4 teaspoons unsalted butter, divided and melted

In a large bowl, beat butter and powdered sugar until light and fluffy. Next, beat in the almond flour and the all-purpose flour.

On a lightly floured surface, roll out the puff pastry to 1/4-inch thick, then cut into an 8-inch circle.

Spray sheet pan with non-stick spray, then place puff pastry on pan.

Spread the almond mixture evenly on top of pastry, leaving a 1-inch border.

Arrange apples in a spiral shape.

Fold over edges of pastry, leaving the middle exposed.

Brush with egg wash and sprinkle the entire galette with cinnamon sugar mixture, then refrigerate for 15 minutes.

Bake in a pre-heated 375-degree oven for 18 to 20 minutes. The pastry will be puffed and golden brown.

Drizzle with butter and serve.

Chocolate Brownies

3 eggs

7 ounces dark chocolate

½ cup granulated sugar

½ cup all-purpose flour

1 pinch ground cinnamon

1 tablespoon brewed coffee

1 cup chopped nuts (optional)

1 ½ tablespoons ground hazelnut

½ cup and 1 tablespoon unsalted butter, softened

Preheat oven to 350 degrees, then grease baking pan and line with parchment paper.

Melt chocolate gently over simmering water, then set aside.

In a bowl, whisk together flour, cinnamon, sugar and hazelnuts. In another bowl, combine eggs, coffee, butter and chocolate.

Combine dry and wet, then pour into dish and bake for 20 to 25 minutes. Let cool for 2 hours.

Raspberry Pistachio Teacakes

1 teaspoon salt

1 ½ cups granulated sugar

1 cup unsalted pistachios, shelled

1 container raspberries

1 stick unsalted butter, softened

4 eggs

2 teaspoons vanilla

1 teaspoon rose water

1 cup all-purpose flour

In a food processor, grind salt, sugar and pistachios into a fine consistency.

Once ground, blend in butter and eggs until well blended.

Once blended, add vanilla, rose water and flour. Blend just until incorporated.

Place in muffin pan with liners and stuff with raspberries and pistachios in between.

Bake in preheated oven at 375 degrees for 28 minutes.

Sugar Cookies

6 ounces unsalted butter, chilled and cut into pieces

½ cup plus 1 tablespoon granulated sugar

¼ teaspoon salt

1 teaspoon vanilla extract

1 ¾ cups all-purpose flour

1 whole egg

Cream butter until pale yellow, then add sugar, salt and vanilla. Cream until light and fluffy.

Add the egg and beat just until incorporated, then fold in flour and chill for 1 hour.

Bake in pre-heated oven at 350 degrees until golden brown.

Holiday Semifreddo

8 ounces mascarpone

1 cup brown sugar

1 cup powdered sugar, sifted

1 stick unsalted butter, melted

½ cup heavy cream

1 cup heavy cream, whipped to stiff peaks

1 teaspoon vanilla

1 teaspoon cloves

1 teaspoon nutmeg

1 teaspoon cinnamon

Mix spices together and set aside.

Combine mascarpone, brown sugar, powdered sugar, butter and the ½ cup of heavy cream and whip until smooth.

Fold in the whipped cream and spices.

Pour into a glass loaf pan lined with plastic wrap and freeze.

Master Lemon Curd

¾ cup granulated sugar

¼ cup fresh lime juice

2 tablespoons lemon zest

3 large eggs

4 large egg yolks

½ cup fresh lemon juice

4 tablespoons (½ stick) unsalted butter, chilled and cut into ½-inch cubes

Prepare an ice bath, using a large bowl to hold the ice.

Fill a medium saucepan ¾ full of water and bring to a simmer over medium heat.

In a food processor, combine sugar and lemon zest, then pulse until the sugar is yellow and fragrant.

In a medium bowl, combine the lemon sugar, eggs and the egg yolks. Whisk for 30 seconds to distribute the sugars (this will keep the eggs from coagulating).

Place the bowl over simmering water and whisk until the sugar is completely dissolved.

Add the lemon and lime juices and cook for 5 minutes whisking continuously, then use a rubber spatula to scrape the sides and the bottom of the bowl periodically.

The curd should have a temperature of 160 degrees and the consistency of sour cream. Transfer into a large bowl, add butter and whisk until the curd is completely mixed and smooth.

Strain curd through cheesecloth, then pour into bowl. Cover with plastic wrap directly on curd so a skin won't form and let cool.

Lemon-Cardamon Pudding Cakes

1 recipe Master Lemon Curd

1 tablespoon all-purpose flour, sifted

½ cup whole milk

3 large egg whites

1/8 teaspoon ground cardamon

1 pinch of cream of tartar

5 tablespoons granulated sugar

To the recipe of curd, add the sifted flour and milk, then whisk until combined. Set aside.

In a separate bowl, whip egg whites at high speed until soft foam appears, then add cream of tartar and cardamon and whip to soft peaks. Lastly, add sugar then whip to stiff peaks.

Using a rubber spatula, carefully fold the egg whites into the curd, a third at a time. 4. Fill ramekins and bake at 300 degrees for 30 minutes. Serve immediately.

DESSERTS

Banana Pudding

1 box vanilla wafers

1 bunch bananas, peeled and sliced

2 pints heavy cream, whipped to stiff peaks

2 cups granulated sugar

1 teaspoon vanilla

6 whole eggs

2 tablespoons all-purpose flour

½ gallon whole milk

Whip heavy cream until stiff peaks, then set aside.

In a heavy saucepan, combine sugar, eggs and flour.

Add milk, then cook over medium heat until thickened for 15 to 20 minutes.

Cool in ice bath; once cooled, fold in whipped cream.

In a glass dish, layer cookies, bananas and cream. Refrigerate for 1 hour.

Caramel Apple Sauce

9 ounces apple juice	In a small bowl, combine water and cornstarch until it makes a slurry, then set aside.
4 ounces granulated sugar	
¼ teaspoon cornstarch	In a small saucepot, beat sugar over medium heat until amber in color. Once amber in color, remove from heat and add apple juice.
1 ounce water	
1 tablespoon unsalted butter	Once apple juice is incorporated, add the slurry, then finish with the butter.
⅛ teaspoon vanilla	Store in air-tight container until use.

Nougat Parfait

2 large eggs	In a medium saucepot, combine water and sugar. Bring to a boil and cook until it reaches 240 degrees.
1 ½ cups heavy whipping cream	In a separate bowl, whip cream until it forms stiff peaks.
1 ¼ cups granulated sugar	Place eggs into a bowl and slowly whisk in the cooked sugar mixture.
¼ cup water	Fold whipped cream into the egg mixture until thoroughly incorporated.
	Refrigerate until ready to be served.

Red Wine Gelee

5 tablespoons cold water	Combine 5 tablespoons of cold water and gelatin in a bowl, then let stand for 5 minutes.
3 tablespoons unflavored gelatin	Combine sugar, ½ water and wine over medium heat. Simmer until sugar is dissolved.
½ cup granulated sugar	
½ cup water	Add gelatin mixture and remove from heat, then pour into strainer onto baking dish and let cool.
2 ¼ cups red wine	Refrigerate uncovered 3 to 4 hours.

Honeycomb Brittle

1 teaspoon baking soda

½ cup granulated sugar

2 tablespoons corn syrup

1 tablespoon honey

2 tablespoons water

Line a baking dish with parchment paper.

Whisk together sugar, corn syrup, honey and water in a saucepan with a candy thermometer.

Heat over medium heat until mixture is thinner, but cloudy. Let bubble and cook until mixture reaches 300 degrees.

Remove from heat. Whisk in baking soda just until incorporated. Switch to a spatula and pour into lined dish but do not spread it out.

Let chill for 30 minutes, then remove paper. Break into pieces and enjoy.

Chocolate Panna Cotta

1 ¼ teaspoons unflavored gelatin

1 ¾ cups heavy cream

2 tablespoons granulated sugar

Pinch of salt

2 ounces bittersweet or semi-sweet chocolate, finely chopped

Pour ¼ cup heavy cream into a small bowl and sprinkle in the gelatin. Let sit until softened. Place that bowl in a bowl of hot water, then stir until dissolved and set aside.

In a saucepan over medium heat, bring the remaining cream, sugar and salt to a boil. 3. Remove from heat, then whisk in the chocolate and gelatin until smooth.

Strain the mixture, then pour into serving dishes.

Cover with plastic wrap and chill.

Libations

Passion Fruit Bellini

16 ounces sparkling wine

4 ounces passion fruit puree

4 dashes thyme syrup

For Thyme Syrup:
1 cup granulated sugar

1 cup water

3 sprigs of thyme

In a chilled pitcher, place passion fruit puree.

Fill with sparkling wine (I prefer a brut cava).

Top with the thyme syrup.

Serve in a champagne flute with a sprig of thyme.

Texas Porch Tea

32 ounces lemonade

10 ounces sweet tea vodka

4 ounces vodka

4 ounces amaretto

1 jar sour cherries, drained

In a chilled pitcher, add lemonade, sweet tea vodka and vodka, then refrigerate for at least two hours.

Before serving, add sour cherries and amaretto.

Serve cold in a Collins glass with a slice of lemon.

Vesper

16 ounces gin

4 ounces vodka

1 bottle of Lillet Blanc Aperitif

2 ounces club soda

In a chilled pitcher, add gin, vodka and lillet.

Top with club soda.

Serve in a martini glass and garnish with an edible flower.

The Hanky Panky

12 ounces gin

12 ounces sweet vermouth

8 dashes Fernet Branca

In a chilled pitcher with ice, add gin, vermouth and Fernet Branca.

Serve in a chilled coupe.

Garnish with a twist of candied orange peel.

Pina Colada

32 ounces Champagne

12 ounces aged rum

12 ounces pineapple juice

6 ounces lime juice

6 ounces Coco Lopez

In a chilled pitcher, add rum, pineapple juice, lime juice and Coco Lopez. Refrigerate until ready to serve.

Before serving, add Champagne.

Serve in pina colada glass.

Garnish with toasted coconut flakes.

Boulevardier

16 ½ ounces rye whiskey

16 ounces Campari

12 ounces sweet vermouth

In a chilled pitcher, add all ingredients.

Serve in rocks glass over ice.

Garnish with pomegranate seeds.

Clover Club

16 ounces gin

4 ounces lemon juice

4 ounces raspberry syrup

4 egg whites

Raspberry syrup:
4 cups sugar

2 cups water

2 cups raspberries

4 tablespoons raspberry jam or preserves

2 ounces vodka

Syrup
Bring syrup ingredients to a boil, then puree, strain and chill.

Syrup
In a chilled pitcher, add gin, lemon juice and syrup.

Refrigerate until ready to serve.

Before serving, whisk in egg whites vigorously.

Serve in highball glass.

The Lady's Spritzer

1 bottle Aperol

1 bottle Prosecco

8 ounces club soda

1 ounce rose water

In a pitcher with ice, add Aperol, club soda and rose water. Chill until serving.

Top with prosecco.

Serve in a champagne flute and garnish with mint.

Daytime Negroni

16 ounces gin

16 ounces Campari

8 ounces vermouth

8 ounces fresh squeezed orange juice

2 ounces tonic water

In a chilled pitcher with ice, add all ingredients and give a gentle stir.

Serve in a rocks glass.

Garnish with a fruit skewer.

www.ingramcontent.com/pod-product-compliance
Lightning Source LLC
Chambersburg PA
CBHW061404010526
44119CB00010B/259